Gabriel FAURÉ

CANTIQUE DE JEAN RACINE

Canticle of Jean Racine
Op. 11 (1865)

edited
with English translation
by

JOHN RUTTER

for SATB chorus and organ, or piano,
or lower strings and harp (see p. 2)

VOCAL SCORE

MUSIC DEPARTMENT

OXFORD
UNIVERSITY PRESS

OXFORD
UNIVERSITY PRESS

Great Clarendon Street, Oxford OX2 6DP, England
198 Madison Avenue, New York, NY10016, USA

Oxford University Press is a department of the University of Oxford
It furthers the University's aim of excellence in research, scholarship,
and education by publishing worldwide

Oxford is a registered trade mark of Oxford University Press
in the UK and certain other countries

Database right Oxford University Press (maker)

© Oxford University Press 1986

23rd impression

This piece has been transcribed by the editor for

violas (minimum 2)
cellos (minimum 2)
basses (minimum 2)
harp

Full scores and instrumental parts are available on hire from the publisher.
An upper voice arrangement (S.S.A.A.) with Fauré's original keyboard accompaniment
is also available (Oxford University Press, ISBN 0 19 342611 0).

This edition of *Cantique de Jean Racine* has been recorded
(together with the Fauré *Requiem*, 1893 version) by the Cambridge Singers
and members of the City of London Sinfonia, conducted by John Rutter, on
Conifer CFRA 122 (cassette MCFRA 122, compact disc CDCFRA 122).

CANTIQUE DE JEAN RACINE

Canticle of Jean Racine

Words by
JEAN RACINE
from *Hymnes traduites*
du bréviare romain
tr. John Rutter

GABRIEL FAURÉ
Op. 11 (1865)
edited by John Rutter

TENORS

No -
Our

No -
our

Verbe é - gal au Très - Haut,
O di - vine Word a - bove,

Printed in Great Britain

OXFORD UNIVERSITY PRESS, MUSIC DEPARTMENT, GREAT CLARENDON STREET, OXFORD OX2 6DP

rom - pons le si - len - - ce, Di - vin Sau -
voi - ces greet the morn - - ing; Look down, O

- veur, jet - - te sur nous les yeux,
Lord, and hear thy peo - ple's prayer,

- veur, jet - te sur nous les yeux,_____ Di -
Lord, and hear thy peo - - ple's prayer,_____ Look

cresc.

B

f   *diminuendo*   *p*

- vin _____ Sau - - veur, jet - te sur nous les
down,_____ O _____ Lord, and hear thy peo - - ple's

f   *diminuendo*   *p*

f   *dimin.*   *p*

31

yeux!
prayer!

il canto marcato

35

pp

39

dolce [C]

Ré - pands   sur   nous   le   feu   de ta
In - spire   us,   Lord,   we   pray,   With the

dolce [C]

12

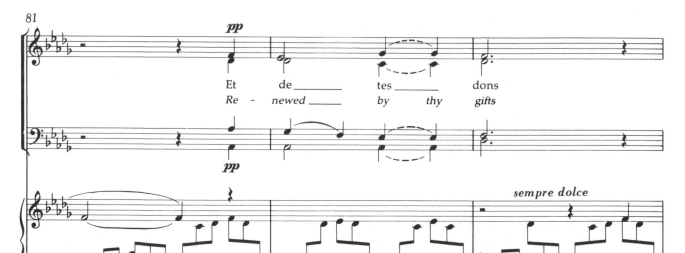